How
the End
First
Showed

WISCONSIN POETRY SERIES

Ronald Wallace, *Series Editor*

D. M. ADERIBIGBE

How
the End
First
Showed

THE UNIVERSITY OF WISCONSIN PRESS

Publication of this book has been made possible, in part, through support from the Brittingham Trust.

THE UNIVERSITY OF WISCONSIN PRESS
1930 Monroe Street, 3rd Floor
Madison, Wisconsin 53711-2059
uwpress.wisc.edu

3 Henrietta Street, Covent Garden
London WC2E 8LU, United Kingdom
eurospanbookstore.com

Printed in the United States of America

This book may be available in a digital edition.

Library of Congress Cataloging-in-Publication Data
Names: Aderibigbe, D. M. (Damilola Michael), author.
Title: How the end first showed / D. M. Aderibigbe.
Other titles: Wisconsin poetry series.
Description: Madison, Wisconsin : The University of Wisconsin Press,
        [2018] | Series: Wisconsin poetry series
Identifiers: LCCN 2018014265 | ISBN 9780299319847 (pbk. : alk.
        paper)
Subjects: | LCGFT: Poetry.
Classification: LCC PR9387.9.A338 H69 2018 | DDC 821/.92—dc23
LC record available at https://lccn.loc.gov/2018014265

for my mother

&

my grandmother

WE ARE VICTIMS OF OUR HISTORY AND OUR PRESENT. THEY PLACE TOO MANY OBSTACLES IN THE WAY OF LOVE. AND WE CANNOT ENJOY EVEN OUR DIFFERENCES IN PEACE.

—Ama Ata Aidoo, *Our Sister Killjoy* (1977)

Contents

SONGS I

SONGS II

AFTER SONGS I

AFTER SONGS II (RECAP)

BEFORE SONGS I

*Of stories, told
and heard.*

QUESTIONS

By the river my grandmother
once failed as a fatherless child,
a young girl

stands with a fish hook
beside her father—planning

to raid a civilization
beneath the river. She ties
a line to the eye of the hook,

drops it into the river.
Inside her father's pupils,

the hook moves—
a line of froth queues
behind, on the water like the trail

of a jet in the sky. She pulls
out the hook,

stuck in the mouth of a fish.
The fish squirms like a flicking finger.
Her father hangs her on his neck

like a winner's medal.
Between that day and this day,

lie questions the two skies
cannot cover: Between the girl
and her father, who caught the fish?

Between my grandmother
and her father, who failed?

OLUMO'S FACE

Walking across a bamboo bridge spread
on a marsh which tore Abeokuta

into two halves, a hoe clipped
to her shoulder, a peg to a cloth

on a line. Shadows of Olumo Rock
fluttering beneath the limbs of insects

perched on the face of the unholy water.
The air stopped moving, but the water

fluttered. My grandmother's eyes
walked on the water.

On the end of the bridge, a man pressed

a woman's head into the water,
because of her dead womb.

When did a woman's failure
lift her to the throne of God

or the seat of Darwin
to give reasons for life?

The man pressed and pressed
her face into the water.

My grandmother, just nine, cried
and cried, before the woman became a ghost.

OEDIPUS

YOU MALES ARE HEARTLESS,
EVEN TO YOUR MOTHERS.

– *Grandma*

To end this brother,
you climbed the moon to a far country
and never came back.
By that I mean, when the police
broke their way into a room,
billowing with suspicion, your body
was a continent of maggots.
By that I mean, when the telephone
brewed with some voice, Mama's
hand went down, fallen skyscraper,
and never came up again, be ni o.
By that I mean, your death
birthed another death.
By that I mean, the neighbors
pleaded with me to unpack
my two bags of grief.
By that I mean, they watched
me dissolve inside their teary eyes.

NEW HELL

Fire burnt on a cold morning:
he screamed *E mi o mo nkankan,*
I'm innocent, until his voice was

swallowed by the ravenous fire.
A woman arrived at the scene
to see her love had become ashes.
She poured tears before a broken
statue of Oshun.
I and my two siblings stood, staring—

our skins veiled by Akure's harmattan.
Police sirens
were a muezzin's voice

that slashed through the morning for solat;

the vigilantes, who made the fire
that melted the life of their thief
without proof he was thief,

dispersed into our bewilderment.
Guns and truncheons lay
on the road, casualties in a war-
torn country. Police
led the new widow to a van.
I and my two siblings stood, staring—

the fire died.

LOVE STORY

AFTER MY GRANDMOTHER

Here's the tale of a woman who spent
many years on the backyard of love:
he burst into her house through the door
like a storm, chased with a gun
by his past. She hid
him inside her deepest secret
where she pasted memories
of heartbreaks: of failed love, of death.
Night stared at them: the two wrapped
in a single blanket in her bed.
The blanket moved and groaned. Morning
spilled on the windowsills and doorway
to her house: he was
gone like the night.

LOVE

Se o ri, this is how your grandfather and I loved—
ni gba ta si wa ni sango ode, so much in love:

in his rickety inheritance, from home we drove
to Bar Beach every evening, where we either made love

or watched a liquid god rise and fall in his salted glory.
Each time, there were those who seemed to be learning if love

was the type of animal that deserved this much attention;
they turned their faces to the gray-suited sky, asking *Dear love,*

are you real, or just something someone somewhere gave a face to?
Back to those of us who believed in the animal called love:

Dami, we were about your age, clenching the beach in our palms;
young enough to believe those sands were tiny children of love.

ELEOS

Lo do do, the day I told
him the hardest part

of being a man,
he came home, trapped in his own heart.
Or should I say, he looked

very much like an adult
in search of adulthood.

There was something about the way
he rested his body on the door,
his eyelashes, waterlogged grasses.

There was something about the way
he went down on his knees,
his palms, lovers kissing.

There was something about the way
he crawled toward me and your mother,
his hands, a pair of gloves I wore.

I had just had your mother,
so loving him again wasn't a task.

THE BEGINNING

AFTER GRANDMA

Omo mi owon, this was how the end first showed:
when he woke up that Wednesday morning,
his teeth were not the lightbulb we had come to know.
Okrika shorts were all he was wearing
when he rode his motorcycle beyond my eye's corner.
Nothing could stop him—not even our one-month-old daughter.

Nothing could stop him, not even our one-month-old daughter
when he rode his motorcycle beyond my eye's corner;
Okrika shorts were all he was wearing.
His teeth were not the lightbulb we had come to know
when he woke up that Wednesday morning—
omo mi owon, this was how the end first showed.

ELEGY FOR MY MOTHERS

FOR GRANDMA, UPON LOSING A FIRST CHILD
June 3, 1976

Let's not pretend the sky
is always plaited with beauty,
even the gods are not perfect.
On my grandmother's skin,
heaven doesn't stop
crying for thirteen years—God's
eyes are patched with red.
A schoolboy's body—
her only son—
empty like a soda can
found at the doorway to his mother's store.
All the women in his life gather
around what the police's anger
has left of him: each calling
his name, as though death
is a disease noise could cure.
Each calls his name,
their breasts flapping like clothes
on a line driven by wind. Lord,
is this what it takes to be a woman?

EASTER NIGHT

AFTER GRANDMA, UPON LOSING A SECOND CHILD
April 25, 1979

A Peugeot 504 sprinted
across the busy night, hitting
your aunt, then a teenage girl
out of my hold.
Voices gathered

around your fallen aunt
like the screams of pastors
casting out demons.
Headlights shone like sun—
a bowl of light beamed on her face; her eyes,

open, yet closed.
The budding twin mountains
on her chest move
like the leafy crown of a mango tree.
The night argued against itself:

a part calling
for doctor's injections and tablets,
a part calling
for elewe omo's herbs and shrubs.
The night argued.

The budding twin mountains
on my girl's chest stopped moving.
I screamed and screamed;
it was Easter.

LAST SUPPER

SO, I FORGAVE YOUR GRANDFATHER WHEN HE CAME
BACK HOME AFTER SIX YEARS (AFTER LOSING TWO OF
OUR CHILDREN), THEN HE LEFT AGAIN AFTER TWO
WEEKS. JUST THREE DAYS LATER, HE CAME HOME AGAIN,
BEGGING, SO I REMINDED HIM OF HIS LAST FEAT.

— *Grandma*

You are sitting in our memory
cross-legged, your left elbow
on the table, right hand

cutting into the mountain
of fufu I made for the night.

Just a punch of the mountain
in your mouth,
I repeat,

just a punch,
you push the table.

The table, a city
in the aftermath of an earthquake.
You rise, walk in the ruins

of my happiness
toward the door.

I hold on to your arm.
Olowo ori mi, I hold
on to your arm,

as one who's afraid of falling
holds on to a tree.

Look, release me, I'm tired
of you, olorun ngbo. You say.
Because love is no longer a god,

when left to one person to worship,
I let go of your arm.

BEFORE SONGS II

*Of stories, told
and heard,
still.*

POTHOS

YOUR FATHER'S MOUTH IS THE SWEETEST EVER.
I EASILY FELL IN LOVE WITH HIM.
— *Mother*

AFTER MY FATHER

Suppose my bones could grow
so long and my flesh
swell so much that heaven
would become my bedroom
and the sky, my floor.
Suppose we humans could
become nothing bigger
than clusters of ants
crawling in corners
and walls of wardrobes.
Suppose I could birth
light and darkness
and my breath could
make a heart function,
I would make my bones
and your blood speak
a common language.

BEFORE ME

They sat on the last row
of an eighteen-seater excitement, loaded
their bags with plantain chips and Agege bread.

The journey started:
Lagos disappeared
into the clear windshield.
The rusted skies of Ibadan bulged—

the journey ended.
A river the natives dreaded
because of the world
at its bed—he stood on its bank,

feeding her promises.
He was yet to spill me into her
then, so she nodded like a lizard.

SONS

My outstretched fingers, flung
toward my sister's cheek.
Poh!! My sister's cheek,

a detonating bomb.
My sleeping mother opened
her eyes. My mother

opened her mouth.
Inside her mouth, the past lay
like a carpet:

inside Ile-Ogbo's mist,
two brothers—my father and uncle—
infected the morning with madness;

their heads, locked against
each other like belligerent rams.
My mother carried my sister,

then a toddler in her arms,
and me a fetus in her stomach.
Our weights too heavy for her,

my mother could not rise
to the height of her
wish, so she screamed

Olowo ori mi, oti to.
So she turned her face
toward her mother-in-law's

window, screaming
again, *Yalegbo, awon mo yin ja.*
My grandmother's window

opened, she looked out:
few villagers were already gathered,
making a movie

of her only sons' madness.
My father was now with a knife,
my uncle with a huge stone.

Each approaching the other
like two trailers with failed brakes.
Both determined to make
their aged mother childless again.

SONGS I

Of witness and memory.

ODE TO MY FATHER'S CHILDHOOD

I woke with my forehead
under your lips, Father.
I followed you into the sloping

street of your childhood. On both sides
of the road, you showed me memories

built with mud, roofed with dry leaves.
We walked further down.

Beside the Ile-Ogbo River,
you told me a secret: this river

once swallowed your cousin
as a person without teeth
swallows a chunk of meat.

Though, the boy was fed
to the river by his parents.

*The boy was useless
since he was born without legs.*
The boy's parents would say.

When did the future
become a see-through window?

You stood and pointed
to a narrow road,
after your fingers, Father,

we moved—now with dusty boots—
deeper into your childhood.

CITY BOY

My father tagged on to the back
of a bus from his village

into prosperity with a pregnant sack
hung to his back like a camel's hump.

The laces of his only footwear
never loosened, my father searched

through job vacancy signboards in Lagos.
The boy outgrew his past, and my mother

would tell his story, days

our plates of food were empty.
On nights we filled our stomachs,

we waited for my father: his shirt
soaked with the day's stress. Sitting

in his armchair, my sister on his left leg,
I on his right, aware those legs

would continue walking
when the sun rose again.

ODE TO YOUR FIRST CRY

FOR OPEYEMI

April 21, 1994

Like the day Jesus was born,
the sky was different that night.
My childhood was packed into many
travel bags. With a truck, we drove
into a better beginning.
Mother's stomach wrapped
around your body, sat on apoti.
Anti mi Bukky and Boda mi Leye
moving all of the past into the future
with bare hands: the black
and white TV, the video
player, Formica-strapped radio,
wall clocks and ceiling fan,
dust and cobwebs,
and the furniture, fragile
like a starving woman.
In a voice borrowed from anger,
mother screamed. The old
woman who sold
agunmu and agbo in the kiosk
beside our new window pulled
off experience from her waist,
wrapped it around mother's thighs,
gbin! She urged.
Between mother's thighs,
a weak cry
rose—your tears brought
us joy, as rain brings to a farmer.

BIRTH

AFTER DILRUBA AHMED

That day, my mother shouted
for her girl. I followed her voice
to the end of the house.
My sweat-soaked mother stretched

my stiffened sister on a mat,
pouring a bottle of aporo,
squeezing a wrap of ata re
into her girl's cold mouth.

Many mothers, few fathers came
after the wounded voice

like ants after sugar. They held God's
neck with their lips. The ghost coughed.
Yes! My sister coughed. People are born
once we know, but she was born twice.

ART OF SURVIVING

AFTER CHIMAMANDA NGOZI ADICHIE

Sunday: tired of God,
I tiptoed out of heaven.
I was just eleven
years old—old enough to sit
on a danfo bus, rolling its tires
on a tiled road leading
to my mother's flabby breasts.
In a market before the street
of my childhood, sounds
flew out of gun-mouths:
the living killing, the living dying;
afternoon dripping of blood.
Behind a building
which never recovered from the crises
that raged on my mother's lips,
I hid beside him; my neighbor,
like me, was dead but breathing.
When the dead finished dying,
we walked with our kneecaps
out of the market like injured soldiers
retreating from a battlefield.
The street was soaked in whispers.
At the entrance to the house,
my half-naked mother
mourned her living son.

MY MOTHER REMAKES THAT MORNING

I

My older sister dragged
me out of a dream.
We placed our ears
on the wall. My father
on the phone, saying *I want you*

to another woman.
My mother heard. She talked and talked.
My father tightened his fists;
my mother's face,
an atlas of injuries.

II

My mother rested
her head on my aunt's arm,
she talked and talked,
remaking the morning
with her tongue like God.

HUNGRY MAN

Aburo mi owon, this was how the day
unfolded from your mouth:
mama mi, ebi npa mi.
Mother peeled and slashed a tuber of yam

to feed three sets of teeth. Blue sun,
hatched from a matchstick burned
beneath mother's ceramic pot.
We salivated; slices of yam softened.

We chewed our teeth; slices of yam perished.
Mother smiled. Father arrived,
filled the room with curses;
his voice beat in our hearts,

as thunder on the walls of a building.
His empty stomach was a bowl of anger.
In a room built with our silence,
father was hitting mother.

TIREDNESS

Vehicles hoot and honk; the deadlocked
traffic jam sputters smoke

into the afternoon. Curses and pleas
sprayed on the road like pollution.

Afternoon gathers around a danfo
bus. Two men struggle to pull

open the door. A man pours his folded
fists on a woman like stones.

I stand outside the bus, looking—
my father slaps and slaps my mother

with the back of his hands.
My mother's lips are broken. Two men

hold up my father's hands, his knuckles
painted with blood. Mother lies on the ground,

tired of rising after every fall.

IN DEFENSE OF LOVE

The morning breathes
sunlight into the room:
my father's robust shadow lies
on the glossy wall beside the bed.
I'm seeing my father
for the first time since we celebrated
the death of the old year.
His face fixed to the TV.
On the TV, the blood of a man splatters
on the bonnet of his car,
while trying to defend the woman he loves.
I gaze at my father.
He wipes tears off his eyes
with the back of his hands.
He turns to me saying
he has ceased being dead.
My mother walks in, carrying
a tray with plates
of efo riro and iyan
from the kitchen, her face
masked with anger. My father
rises above the tray in my mother's
hands, his fingers all over her head—
on my mother's face, agony dies.

BECOMING MY MOTHER'S SON

The morning sun in the room
lightened a secret that slipped
out of his drunken pocket.
My mother packed all of her devotion
into two travel bags; she strapped
my little sister to her back
with her gele, tightened her hand
around my wrist like a wristband.
My father fastened his fingers
around my other wrist,
and they fought over my life:
he with punches, my mother with tears.
Mo fe ba moimi lo. I cried.
My father released my wrist.
I watched him fold the love
he had for me in his right hand,
never to unfold that hand again.

TO BE MY FATHER

February 20, 2000

My mother's purse rang,
her hand to her ear:
my father's voice,
a threatening thunder.
My mother rushed all of her hopes
into the store and locked
the evening with a huge padlock.
She held my hand, we boarded
a danfo bus. A hospital,
a doctor, two nurses. My mother
dropped her purse on my lap,
went into a room with them.
A doctor, two nurses, they came
out and told me to fill their past
with my footprints. In the room:
my mother on a bed, her eyes
shut like death.
Her lower lip held between her teeth,
a peg holding a shirt. Blood trickled
like tears from her skirt, ran
across her legs.
I was ten,
but I knew what it took
to be my father was to cause
a woman's pain.

REMAKING THE DAY

She stood at the entrance
like a gatekeeper, the knob
of the door to my parents'
marriage in her hand like an egg.
She spat out my father's name.

My father worshipped her voice:
he rushed to the wardrobe,
folding his promises, arranging
them inside a travel bag.
She stepped out of the room;
my father's hand in her hand.

The travel bag rolled
behind them. My mother—her lips
warm with my father's
goodbye—stood still like a pillar.
The afternoon's yellow eye, a furnace.
But in my mother's eyes, the sky

was a blanket of water.

MIRROR

We watched the gap in her teeth
when she boasted of their future:

they moved the television,
the video, the chairs, the carpet,

even Nelson Mandela was pulled
from the wall and placed inside

their last child's backpack. They did
not stop—until they compressed

their memories into a truck.
They left the doors and windows

unlocked. The truck drove off. I peeked.
Found only a mangled mirror.

I sat before it, staring
clearly at my past in broken shapes.

All that had come and gone: my toy plane
which crashed inside the neighbor's

kitchen, my water gun, broken
by my sister's boyfriend,

and my father, who I was
seeing again through this mirror.

SEPARATING FROM MY FUTURE

I sit at the foot of my aunt's house.
The rest of my bloodline gathers
around a telephone,

waiting to hear another set
of my father's snowy lies from Milan.
On the sunny ground

before me, there is my shadow—
my father's past—gawking
at me with blank eyes: a past

I would feed to some hungry gods in place
of a return to my mother's womb.

My mother and her sister
joke of their slow death,
about their murderous men.

Their footsteps sound louder.
In a minute, I'll see
their dying faces;

Lord, how do I tear
my future out of these veins
running across my life?

IN PRAISE OF
OUR ABSENT FATHER

On the fifth day of a month
made of harmattan and cold sun,
my mother washed dirt off grains of rice.

She chopped carrots, onions, pepper,
and liver on a slab into rings.

My older sister slit open
the belly of a huge eja kote—
packed out its intestine as one offloads

clothes from a bag. Beads of sweat
slipped down their faces.
The sitting room: strands of Juju

melody streamed out of the stereo—
the house was covered with music.
From the kitchen: my mother's efforts smelled

delicious. My mother wore
aso-oke—she danced, we ate—
raising cups in praise of her loneliness.

THE CLEANER

Saturday morning:
you wipe the dust
on the furniture out of living
with a towel, erase the week's

feet with a mopping stick
and soapy water.
You pull out a stack
of his clothing from the wardrobe

as a yam farmer harvests tubers
from the rewarding ground
and straighten the clothes
with a pressing iron.

You pull out the last letter
he wrote before eloping
with the Swedish woman.
The day gets hotter:

you pull him out
of a photo album;
he smiles at us
from your palms, we smile

back. Mother, you push
the picture to your chest—
patting and patting
what's left of my father.

PINK

Because my father dips himself
into the vagina of a Swedish woman

and is never found again,
my mother's heart dies.

I follow her as a chick follows
the hen it sees when crawling out of a hatched egg.

My sister follows her like a goat with a rope
fastened around its neck. We follow

my mother into her new love. My sister,
seeing the clouds walk across the moon

from the window of her new fate,
turns her face to me;

her eyes, those of a woman
in labor of childbirth.

I stopped pressing the pads
of an electronic bribe

the new man gave for my mother's
nightly noise. My sister walks

toward me; my sister's left hand
walks on my skinny cheek.

Oluwa mi oo, my sister's left
hand colors my mood into the pink

of her palms. The pink of her palms, drenched
with tears over the death of our parents' love.

MISSING

How much commitment
does it take to keep love
from deteriorating
to a wilted flower?

On a Sunday
afternoon heated with God's eye, Father,
you wrote a story on my mother's
skull with a corkscrew

before leaving for Milan.
The story stretched
between her cornrows. She hid
loneliness under her

blanket every night.
The fifth year after you left,
another man took her into his skin.

How long can a one-legged
woman stand without crutches?
When my sister had become
a teenager, her phone rang;

she stuck the phone to her ear.
On the end of the line
was you, Father, begging.

How much muscle can a river
muster to sweep back a golden pendant
that got drowned many years before?

CHRISTMAS WISHES

December 20, 2004, Abadan

We were outside,
because we were young.
Because my father's
white tongue was travelling
around the body of his new woman.
Above our heads, Christmas
shattered into shining pieces.
The city was lost inside the voices
of excited children.
I picked up a pen,
began drawing my two Christmas
desires on a paper.
After, I posted my heart
to a wall and stared at it. Knowing
if only I were a god
who could make wishes breathe,
I and my sisters would be dancing
with Santa's gown.
Behind us, my father would roam
around my mother's nostrils.

LEARNING MY HISTORY

AFTER NATASHA TRETHEWEY

At twelve, on one
of the days outside the surface
of my skin, you drove
me through the streets of your regrets
in your new husband's Volkswagen.
Pointing left and right like a tree's
swaying branch, as dust covered
your mistakes. You drove
on, arrived at the house
you fell in love with the history
that is now mine. Alighting
from the car, I followed
you like a good name, Mother. Mother,
on the soil where he planted
me on your lips,
I watched the sun slice
you into two, your heart.

DANCING

FOR IYANUOLUWA
December 5, 2008

The day starts in my little sister's
little fingers: her fingers,

cupped around an apple.
Her teeth sink into it—

her mouth dances and dances,
like I danced. Lord! I danced

when the news walked into the room
that she had been forced

out of my mother's stomach
with the doctor's knife.

Lord! I danced when my mother's
stomach was sewn back together.

Lord! I danced when I saw,
yes! I saw our anxiety wrapped

in a white shawl, beside my mother.

SONGS II

Of witness and memory, still.

IN DEFENSE OF SILENCE

When typhoid fever struck,
you became a toddler.

Clouds drew across the sky,
dark windowpanes.

I cried as I watched the day
kill you slowly.

The neighbors came. One of them
poured his voice into his phone.

Not long after, an ambulance came.
Not long after, I sat

beside the bed you were laid. A nurse
drew blood from your arms

with a syringe. A stethoscope lay
on the entrance to your life.

I sat above your fate: your fingers
in mine. Goose pimples

all over your body. You shivered
and shivered like a chicken

with soaked feathers, calling
the name of God. I was silent,

like any child who knew
the day of his mother's death.

So silent that my heartbeats were
sounds of gunshots in a battlefield.

MATRICULATION DAY

I wake with the previous night
stuffed in my heart—
the news of my admission
into the university;
three-year-old depression,
killed by a day-old happiness.
Doesn't celebration start with a day?
My happy mother can't celebrate.
She lays sickly on the bed
like a wire, her rich flesh ruined
by an ambitious sickness:
my eyelashes, skirts brought
out of a stream.

BEFORE THE ELEGIES

It was the last time I stepped into your bedroom,
I remember. You could hardly complete the name
you gave me, but I moved closer to the thin frame
of sheets on your bed. I should have known what loomed,
after all, your legs had run out of muscles
for a week now. Stupid me, I thought miracles

cost nothing. I pulled off the sheet, the day's
legacy all over your thighs. On your bed,
a map of orange-red odor. *Bathroom* you said.
Ah! How easily the body betrays
the mind. Two weeks ago, it was you alone, hacking
down grasses that invaded the backyard. Clutching

a cutlass, then a hoe, cutlass, hoe, cutlass.
You had never waited on anyone
until this week, this day! As a good son,
I put you in my arms, light as a shard of glass.
My mouth, a cannon of promises: I swore
you wouldn't be by yourself again. I shut the door

to the bathroom, once I had let you sit.
Soap on your head, I began to wash away my guilt.

FINAL TURN

December 2, 2020, Emure-Ekiti

The sun broke in through
the pores on the panes of the windows—

a new day. I do house chores: clean yesterday's
fingers out of the plates, spoons, and cups.

Sweep out legs made of sand
from the apartment.

The rest in the house are spirits:
you, your sister, and her husband. The morning's

task, pushed into my past,
I call, and you turn human:

yawning and stretching on your bed.
I button up my shirt,

zip up my pants and wear sunglasses
over my fears; set for classes.

My schoolbag stuck to my back,
my outstretched fingers wave

like blades of a standing fan.
I step into God's bright gaze. My name

wrapped inside your sick voice:
I turn my head back to you,

my last duty as your son.

AFTER SONGS I

Elegies.

LAST CALL

AFTER CHLOE HONUM
December 2, 2020, Lagos

We argued: I and Uche, emptying
our thoughts into the inglorious
future our fathers mapped out for us.
Aren't these men supposed to be our heroes

instead of their women? We'd ask.
The pocket where I kept my mother's
dying face when I departed
Emure-Ekiti vibrated:

Come home now now,
it's about your mother oo.
The voice commanded. I ran.
Running on a track filled

with ranges of trees.
Leaves bent and rose
like Muslims in prayer.
It rained. Raining.

I ran. Running. Home;
the flaming butt of a cigarette,
the only light in the living room.
My step-father's voice spread
into the darkness; my mother

lost an eternal battle.
My step-father spread more darkness—
his courage, soaked in tears,
and then he apologized.

LAST FOREVER

December 2, 2020

Say these bones were stones,
would my mother leave her bed
for a wooden box covered with dirt
and sealed with cement?

You were a caricature
of yourself—drawn with tears—
when you stood at the door, asking
me how it happened. You did

not become what I could touch
until you rubbed your chest
against mine on the couch.
You took me out of the house, leaving
behind my sisters, who were crowding

the house with the names of my mother.
On the road, everything
was still made of water:
the cars, the motorcycles, buildings.
You told stories, your voice died trying

to find routes into my ears. You dipped
a handkerchief into my eyes, drying
away bitter memories
with your kindness. A truck moved

toward us, its headlights bright
like morning's flesh. You told me to keep
my eyes on the sleek covet;
I saw a reflection of light

run through it briefly. The truck
went into a dark distance. You asked
if the reflection lasted forever.
Your lips, a language my cheek understood.

I stood by the roadside like a tree,
you got small, smaller,
till you became the darkness
that helped me to see.

LUNCH TIME

News of my mother's death
on the day's tongue.
I flip through an album
of her pictures.

My sister is a mother at two—
she feeds her doll
from the footprints of well-wishers
who have come to share our grief.

My brother pedals his bicycle;
skidding up and down the street.
Sun shines from his head.

My step-father fixes
a cigarette into his mouth—
smokes out of his nostrils.
His eyes, glowing embers.

The voice on the radio says
2 pm—time for lunch.
The dining room is an empty stadium.

I peek into my mother's bedroom:
her pillow lies at the center of the bed.

OUT OF WATER

December 3, 2010

It was the sound
machines make
that tore
out of my grandmother's
mouth when her dreams
grew flesh: her first daughter
became her ancestor.
The night
folded around her face;
she left to lie
in moon's palms, by the road.
Her eyelashes brut like leaves
in a Lagos
afternoon.
A woman walked
under my grandmother's feet,
wearing her children's
hands on her waist
like multiple belts—
her hands on their shoulders.
They walked
across my grandmother's
body: mother and children,
laughing and laughing.
My grandmother's eyes
on their back:
their bodies, made of water.

MOTHER, AGAIN

The bus drives me into nostalgia:
the window, the clouds gathering

around the sky. Evening dies
slowly; Lagos, lost in dusk's huge frame.

The bus park's halogen lamps lighten the night.
At the junction where I planted you

for the last time on my back, Mother, I sell my body

for a vase of flowers, for a bottle of nail polish.
I ply the road to the deteriorating

wall of your grave, where I inscribe
the debt I owe you with a brush

drenched with nail polish. I set
a vase upon your concrete breasts.

ART OF UNLEARNING

December 2, 2013

I look out through the window
of my step-father's house—
straight at my mother's
grave, wondering if I could
ever unlearn that afternoon:
if I could unwrite the epitaph.
If the bricklayer could unmould
the grave's slabs. If the boys
who filled the grave
could pack out the dirt.
If the fistful of dirt could return
to my fists. If the pastor's prayers
could retreat into his mouth.
If the undertakers could bring
out her coffin from the grave,
place it on their shoulders,
walk backward, and drop
it in the hearse. If the hearse
could move in reverse.
If tears could snake
back into my eyes. If the diggers
could fill back the pit
that became my mother's grave
with that heap of dirt
which stood in front of me,
an unwanted rock.

AFTER SONGS II
(RECAP)

Of stories heard and witnessed.

OUR LEGEND

December 18, 2013, Akure

At night, inside the reflection
of a halogen lamp,
I told my younger siblings
a story about our dead mother.
I told the story, my siblings swayed
on a swing: forward and backward.
Backward: my mother told a story
to me; when I was a baby—
my life wrapped in a shawl,
I lay beside my mother.
She told a story to my father
about his other woman.
He lifted up a stool like a trophy,
the stool on my mother's
head, our parents' love crashed
like the framed photo of their marriage
for the first time. As my mother
told this story to me, I was swaying
on a swing backward and forward.
Forward: at night, inside the reflection
of a halogen lamp,
I told my younger siblings this story
of the past that became us.

ODE TO MY
GRANDMOTHER'S MOUTH

My grandmother's voice replaced
the day when the sun died.
My cousin hatched
a matchstick, rounded
fire over the threads
of a kerosene stove:
water boiled. My cousin stirred
a bowl of elubo lafun
in the steaming
pot with a pestle. My grandmother
ate; she sang my cousin's oriki.
My grandmother,
her mouth a wrinkled tunnel
leading to more stories: of a girl
who ate two apples
and became pregnant;
of pregnancy
which grew not knowing
what the touch of a father
felt like; of vagina
which spilled my sister
into the palms of no man.

A FULFILLED CHILDHOOD

The sun has fallen
upon the pawpaw trees like sawdust
on a woodcarver; it feeds
greenness with scorching sunlight.

The cocks crow and chickens chirp
under the roofs. Lizards
on fences seek to crush
our undying favor for breakfast.

Songs from speakers have
taken the street. The revving
of motorcycles and vehicles
has taken the road.

Now that I have no other place to go,
I'll go into my grandmother's fingers,
wrap myself with her blanket,
pick a sheet of paper and a pen,

and I'll rewrite my childhood.
Amputating my father's hands
and legs with ink, like rebels
chop innocuous civilians. By god,

my childhood will lack nothing.
Nothing at all.

CONFESSION OF
A HUNGRY SON

Father, before I begin, forgive
my mouth, for it had let your name
burn to ashes:
the week fell on mother's
shoulders like a wall.
She took cheap pills, bought
from an apothecary.
She lay in her bed like a grave,
drew the blanket
over herself like cobwebs
across a ceiling. The afternoon
crawled in our starving stomachs.
Our fingers combed
and combed mother's secrets.
When nothing was found,
we carved a hole
inside her ears with our voices;
but what difference would a pin
make if inserted into the skin
of the dead? His white shoe stepped
into the room like the sun—his hands,
filled with our dreams.
Father, we sold
you because of the hunger you left
for us to watch over; my sisters
and I sold you for three plates of rice
and fried chicken.
Baa mi, I'm sorry—your cubs
lived in a ship-pen for ten years.

PRODIGAL

A junior student rushed
out of the principal's office,
my name billowing out of his mouth
like a divulged secret, while it rained.
It rained, but the boy's voice
was louder than god's,
so it took me less time
to run from the football field
to the principal's office
than a bullet would take
to take a life. Shocked,
like a victim of a stray bullet,
I looked; my father sitting
on a couch, his hair, gray with neglect.
Baba mi, Baba mi.
He turned his head to me,
then ran after his own gaze.
Omo mi, omo mi, look at you.
He held me—gathering
lost years with both hands.

COLORS OF MY CHILDHOOD

I BELIEVE IN CHILDHOOD, A NATIVE LAND OF MATH
EXAMS THAT RETURN AND DO NOT RETURN
— *Ilya Kaminsky*

The school term lodged in my past,
you drove us to a field full

of childishness: some riding
electronic horses, some playing

computer games. I asked
for a story, spiced

only with your childhood.
You gaped at the sparkling floor,

the reflection of a man tortured
by a tough childhood gaped

back: the cup of ice cream in your hand,
a thawing snow. I would lose

you to snows years later: Milan,
Stockholm, and Amsterdam.

And my mother would go from town
to town in search of a husband

who was neither dead nor alive.
On good days, I'll ask her,

could there ever be a boy's childhood
built outside his father's

shadow? My mother
could not outlive this question.

If my son requests to see
my distant past, Father,

do you ever wonder
what color it would appear?

Acknowledgments

Gratitude to the publications (online and print) in which these poems or previous versions of them appeared: "Oedipus," *The Nation*; "Confession of a Hungry Son;" *Prairie Schooner*; "Olumo's Face," *Alaska Quarterly Review*; "Ode to Your First Cry," *Colorado Review*; "To Be My Father," Mirror," *The Normal School*; "City Boy," *Poet Lore*; "Separating from My Future" (as "Hero"), *Notre Dame Review*; "Our Legend," *Salamander*; "Art of Unlearning," *Amazon's Day One*; "Art of Surviving," *RHINO*; "Hungry Man" (as "Cannibal"), *African American Review*; "Questions," *Hotel Amerika*; "Remaking the Day," *Spillway*; "Mother, Again," *Asheville Poetry Review*; "Pink," "Out of Water," *Hobart*; "Elegy for My Mothers," *Apogee Journal*; "Easter Night," *Folio*; "Tiredness," *Weave Magazine*; "In Praise of Our Absent Father," *Connotation Press*; "Dancing," *Grist*; "Lunch Time," *Arsenic Lobster*; "Ode to My Grandmother's Mouth," *Mead*, 2014 reprinted by *Poetry Society of America*; "A Fulfilled Childhood," *B O D Y*; "New Hell," *Vinyl Poetry*; "Love Story," *Fjords Review*; "My Mother Remakes That Morning," *Juked*; "Missing," *Ostrich Review*; "Last Call," *Prime Number*; "The Cleaner," "Sons," *Hawai'i Review*; "Matriculation Day," *DIAGRAM*; "Last Forever," *Ampersand Review*; "Birth," "Becoming My Mother's Son," *The Cortland Review*; "Learning My History," *Past Simple*; "Ode to My Father's Childhood," "Colors of My Childhood," *Natural Bridge*; "Christmas Wishes," *River Styx*; "Before Me," *Yemassee Journal*; "Pothos," *PANK*; "Last Duty" (as "Final Turn"), *Small Orange*.

Some of the poems have also appeared in a chapbook titled *In Praise of Our Absent Father*, published by Akashic Books and APBF.

I give thanks to God for the strength to write this book.

I'm grateful to the editors and staff of the University of Wisconsin Press for guiding me through the publication process with love and patience.

I'm grateful to the following foundations for offering me residencies and fellowships to work on this book: the James Merrill House, Jentel Foundation, OMI International Arts Center/Ledig House, and Ucross Foundation.

I'm eternally grateful to Aimee Nezukhumatathil for her generosity and close attention to my work. Likewise, I'm eternally grateful to Ron Wallace and other faculty members at the University of Wisconsin–Madison's Institute for Creative Writing for their attention to my work.

I'm grateful to my teachers at Boston University for their guidance and vision. I'm grateful to my high school literature teacher at Queen's Science and Arts Secondary School, Suleja: Uncle T for being my first ever writing teacher.

I'm grateful to the African Poetry Book Fund family for their unending support.

I'm grateful to my poetry forerunners and peers who accepted me into their folds: Jack Campbell, Phil Brady, Steve Reece, Francesca Bell, Lena Gronlund, Chloe Honum, Nayelly Barrios, Gbenga Adesina, Nandini Dhar, J. Scott Brownlee, Chris Crawford, Joshua Mensch, Andre Bagoo, Laura Kaminski, and Ejiofor Ugwu.

I'm grateful to my Unilag friends who became family: Lanre Awode, Emmanuel Esan, Tosin (Threxx), Abayomi Gbade-Bello, Ezekiel Oyebade, Kunlexzy, Wale "Wagy" Lawal, Seun Sholeye, Mayowa Otuseso, Olaitan Balogun, and Atunde Olabisi.

I'm grateful to my Agege family—awon temi, awon ti ema komi-je bi indomie: Teniola Tonade, Demilade Oyelakun, and Lekan.

I'm grateful to The Weavers for giving me that much-needed home on campus: Kayode Odumboni and Samuel Olatunji.

I'm grateful to Kayode Odumboni again and Ayo for letting me use their computers to finish the first draft of this manuscript when I didn't have one.

I'm grateful to my Ikorodu friends who became family: Ike-chukwu Emeahu, Bernard Iregbu, Ahmed Adebayo, Ebenezer Adegbule, and Abu Adebayo—ele nu pa!

I'm grateful to my Suleja friends who became family: Kayode Adekunle (bestie of life), Marcel Orukpe, and Victor Idialu.

I'm grateful to my Boston friends who became family: Biodun Olaoye, Obe Okaiwele, Manelisi Victor Nlhiziyo, Aubrey Dube, Ines Ouadraogo, Amadou Barrow, and Christian Mamo.

I'm eternally grateful to the Oristaglios and Aunt J for treating me like family.

I'm again grateful to my Mama O for making my life livable. What a mother you are!

I'm eternally grateful to Shilpi Suneja and her venerable mother, Ms. Neena Wahi, for treating me like family

Again, I'm eternally grateful to Shilpi for helping me up each time I fell.

I'm grateful to Pastor Taiwo Olarinde for his spiritual support.

Last but obviously not the least, I'm grateful to my family for their endless prayers: Aderibigbes, Adegbites, Adenijis, Babalolas, Akandes, Oshos, Adewales, Makanjus—eni yan la so mi.

Lastly, I am deeply sorry if I omitted any names here, I am only human and the mind is bound to fail sometimes. *Thank you.*

WISCONSIN POETRY SERIES

Ronald Wallace, *Series Editor*

(B) = Winner of the Brittingham Prize in Poetry
(FP) = Winner of the Felix Pollak Prize in Poetry
(4L) = Winner of the Four Lakes Prize in Poetry